FUNNY ANIMALS OF THE WORLD JOKE BOOK
for kids

WONDERFUL WORLD OF ANIMALS BOOK 4

JACK LEWIS

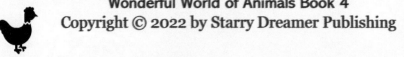

Funny Animals of the World Joke Book for Kids
Wonderful World of Animals Book 4
Copyright © 2022 by Starry Dreamer Publishing

For information contact:
Starry Dreamer Publishing
LLC 1603 Capitol Ave. Suite 310 A377
Cheyenne, Wyoming 82001
starrydreamerpub@gmail.com

Written by Jack Lewis
Photo Credits: All images contained herein are used under license from Shutterstock.com (See Index for complete list)
Front Cover Photo Credits:
Blue Iris, Jaana Piira, JIFF, Nagel/Shutterstock
Back Cover Photo Credits:
Sergey Novikov, Vasily Sminov/Shutterstock

ISBN: 978-1-952328-72-5 (Hardcover) 978-1-952328-73-2 (Paperback)
Library of Congress Cataloging-in-Publication Data is available
10 9 8 7 6 5 4 3 2 1
First Edition: August 2022

STARRY DREAMER PUBLISHING

Cheetah

FUN FACT
Unlike other large cats, cheetahs cannot roar!
Instead, one might hear them hiss, chirp,
growl, or purr like a housecat!

What do you get when you
cross a burger and a cheetah?
FAST FOOD!

Which is the fastest kind of cheetah?
THE ONE ON ROLLER SKATES.

What do cheetahs have on each foot?
Cheetoes.

Parrot

What's a parrot's favorite game?

HIDE-AND-SPEAK!

What do you get when you cross a parrot with a shark?
A bird that will talk your ear off!

A man walked into a pet shop looking to buy a new pet and saw a parrot with a string attached to each leg.

He asked what the strings were for, and the shopkeeper replied, "Well, if you pull the right string, the parrot says, 'Polly wanna cracker,' and if you pull the left string, it says, 'My name is Fred.'"

The man thought for a moment and asked, "What happens if I pull both strings at the same time?"

The parrot piped up, "I'd fall off the perch, you dummy!"

Deer

FUN FACT
Some species of deer can run up to 40 miles per hour and jump over 10 feet high!

What does a deer use to clean its feet?
Hoof-paste!

Who did the deer invite to her birthday party?
HER *DEER*-EST FRIENDS!

Which animal is a fan of wet weather?
A rain-deer.

Donkey

FUN FACT
Believe it or not, a donkey is stronger than a horse of the same size!

What has six legs, four eyes, two heads, and a tail?

A human sitting on a donkey.

A man in a movie theater notices what looks like a donkey sitting next to him.

"Are you a donkey?" asked the man, surprised.

"Yes."

"What are you doing at the movies?"

The donkey replied, "Well, I really liked the book."

Cat

FUN FACT
Cats have an extra organ on the roof of their mouth that lets them taste smells in the air!

What do polite cats say after they burp?
Paw-don me! I'm *furry* sorry!

What's a cat's favorite cereal?
Mice crispies.

What color do kitties love the most?
Purrrrrrple.

If lights run on electricity and cars run on gas, what do cats run on?
Their paws.

Gecko

FUN FACT
Geckos have a funny way of escaping predators. They will drop their tail, run away, then regrow a new one!

WHY ARE GECKOS NATURAL-BORN STORYTELLERS?
Dropping a <u>tail</u> is in their nature!

WHAT DO YOU CALL A GECKO WHO KNOWS MAGIC?
A lizard wizard!

WHAT DO GECKOS LIKE TO EAT WITH THEIR HAMBURGERS?
French flies!

Horse

What does it mean when you find a horseshoe?
Somewhere a horse is walking around wearing just a sock!

Where do horses go when they're sick?
The *horse*-pital!

A man is walking through the country when he spots a sign that reads, "Talking Horse for Sale." Curious he walks up to the stable to check it out and sees the horse and its owner.

"Can you really talk?" he asks the horse.

"I sure can!" the horse miraculously answers. "And I can also play the violin!" he adds.

Amazed the man questions the owner, "Why on earth would you want to get rid of such an incredible animal?"

The owner replies, "Because he's a liar! He can't play the violin!"

Koala Bear

FUN FACT

Eucalyptus leaves are poisonous to humans and most animals, but they are a koala's favorite food! Koalas eat up to 1.5 pounds of the toxic leaves a day!

What's small, furry, and slightly purple?
A koala holding its breath!

What do you call a koala bear with no teeth?
A gummy bear!

Besides eucalyptus leaves, what is a koala bear's favorite vegetable?
Koala-flower!

Tapir

FUN FACT

A tapir's trunk is really an extended upper lip and nose they use to grip branches and strip them of leaves or to help them pluck yummy fruit!

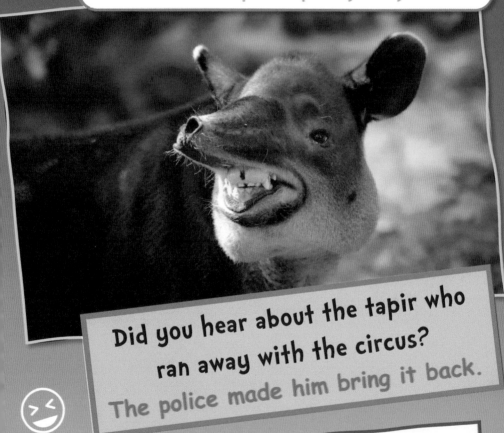

Did you hear about the tapir who ran away with the circus?

The police made him bring it back.

WHY DID THE BABY TAPIRS GET KICKED OUT OF THE POOL?

Their trunks kept falling down!

Wolf

WHAT DO YOU CALL A WOLF WITH A FEVER?
A hot dog!

Did you hear about the wolf that couldn't stop laughing?

HE THOUGHT EVERYTHING WAS *HOWL*-ARIOUS!

Little Red Riding Hood is walking alone through the forest to her grandmother's house. She hears a rustling in the bushes and investigates. When she pokes her head through the leaves, she sees a giant wolf sitting on a log.

"Are you The Big Bad Wolf?" she nervously asks.

The surprised wolf growls in a deep voice, "Yes, I am!"

Little Red runs away as fast as she can until she's out of breath. Soon she calms down, finds the path again, and cautiously continues her way through the woods. A few minutes later, she hears another noise. This time it's coming from behind a group of trees. Curious, she peers around a tree trunk only to come nose to nose with the giant wolf squatting in front of her.

"Are... are you the same Big Bad Wolf?" she gasps in fright.

The wolf lets out a howl. "Yes, I AM," he snarls. "Now, will you go away and leave me alone? I'm trying to poop here!"

Mole

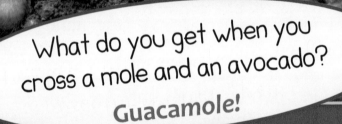

What do you get when you cross a mole and an avocado?

Guacamole!

What fruit do moles love to eat in the summer?
Water-molens!

How do you stop a mole from digging holes in your lawn?
Take away his shovel!

16

Snowy Owl

WHAT IS A SNOWY OWL'S FAVORITE HOLIDAY?
Owl-oween!

What did the snowy owl order at the ice cream shop?
A HOOT-beer float.

What do you get if you cross kittens and owls?

Meowls!

Chimpanzee

FUN FACT
Chimps are so intelligent they can learn human sign language! A chimpanzee named Washoe learned over 350 words in sign language!

Why was the jungle party so lame?
Somebody forgot to bring the *chimps* and dip!

What is a chimp's favorite Christmas carol?
 Jungle Bells!

What kind of monkey likes seafood?
A *shrimpanzee.*

A policeman in the big city stops a man in a car with a chimpanzee sitting in the front passenger seat.

"What are you doing with that chimpanzee?" the policeman asks. "You should be taking it to the zoo."

The following week, the same policeman spots the same man with the chimp again in the front seat, and they're both wearing sunglasses.

The policeman pulls him over. "I thought I told you to take that chimpanzee to the zoo!" he yells.

The man replies, "I did. He had such a good time that now he wants to visit the beach!"

Dog

What kind of dog did Dracula have?
A bloodhound.

Where do dogs hate to shop?
At flea markets.

What snack do dogs get at the movies?
Pup-corn!

Cow

Knock, knock.
Who's there?
Cows go.
Cows go who?
No, cows go moo!

What do you get from a cow during an earthquake?
A milkshake!

What do cows bring to math class?
Cow-culators!

Goat

What is a little goat's favorite nursery rhyme to sing?

"ROW, ROW, ROW YOUR GOAT."

22

DID YOU HEAR ABOUT THE AMAZING GOAT WHO CAN PAINT?

His name is Vincent Van Goat!

Knock, knock.

Who's there?

Goat.

Goat who?

Goat to the door and see who it is!

Raccoon

What kind of stories do raccoons like?

Furry tails.

How can you tell two raccoons apart?

You can't, they're both wearing masks.

What is a raccoon's favorite type of car?

Furarris!

Rabbit

How do you know carrots are good for your eyes?
Because you never see rabbits wearing glasses!

Where do rabbits go after their wedding?
On their bunnymoon!

What kind of books do rabbits like to read?
The kind with hoppy endings!

Dolphin

What do dolphins
need to stay healthy?
Vitamin Sea!

Why did the dolphin cross the road?
To get to the other tide!

WHERE DO DOLPHINS GO TO SLEEP?
In their water beds!

Why can dolphins only live in salt water?
Because pepper water makes them sneeze!

Macaque

HOW DO YOU CATCH A MONKEY?
Climb a tree and act like a banana.

Why don't macaques wear suspenders?
Because they don't wear pants!

Did you hear about the macaque who started her own company?
She was good at monkey business!

28

Lion

FUN FACT
Do you know how loud a lion can be? A lion's booming roar can be heard up to 5 miles (8km) away!

Knock, knock.
Who's there?
Lion.
Lion who?
I'm lyin' here waiting for you to open the door!

On which day do lions eat the most?
Chewsday!

Why did the lion spit out the clown?
He tasted funny!

Elephant

Why are elephants so wrinkly?
Well, have you ever tried to iron one?

How can you tell that elephants are always ready for an adventure?

They've always got their trunks ready to go!

Because when you climb into bed, your nose touches the ceiling.

Wallaby

What's a wallaby's favorite candy?
Lolli-hops!

Did you hear about the dizzy marsupial?
It was a wobbly wallaby.

Sea Turtle

FUN FACT
Unlike other turtles, sea turtles cannot retract their head and flippers into their shells!

What type of turtles are easiest to spot?
Green SEE turtles.

What do sea turtles do on their birthday?
THEY *SHELL*-EBRATE!

What is a sea turtle's favorite sandwich?
Sea-nut butter and jellyfish.

Zebra

Why is it so difficult to sell a toy zebra?

YOU CAN NEVER FIND THE BARCODE.

WHAT DO ZEBRAS HAVE THAT NO OTHER ANIMAL HAS?
Baby zebras, of course!

Who would win in a fight between a zebra and a kangaroo?

The zebra because he has so many black belts!

Brown Bear

What is a bear's favorite type of pie?
Blue-bear-y!

What is a bear's favorite drink?
A root bear float.

What color socks do
brown bears wear?
None. They usually walk
around with <u>bear</u> feet.

Water Dragon

Knock, knock.
Who's there?
Dragon.
Dragon who?
I'm dragon today
and could use a nap.

What types of stories are water dragons famous for?
Long **tales!**

Why are water dragons such great musicians?
BECAUSE THEY KNOW THEIR *SCALES!*

Crocodile

What's worse than one crocodile chasing you?

TWO crocodiles chasing you!

Who brings presents to little crocodiles at Christmas?

Santa Jaws!

What do you get when you cross a rooster and a crocodile?

A croc-a-doodle-doo!

Cape Buffalo

FUN FACT
Cape buffalo may be massive, but they are excellent swimmers and can easily cross an entire river in search of better grazing!

What time is it when a buffalo sits on your bed?
Time to get a new bed!

What do you call a buffalo at the North Pole?
Very lost!

What is as big as a buffalo but weighs nothing?
Its shadow.

39

Sloth

One day a sloth was robbed by three turtles.

When the cops showed up to help him, they asked, "What did the turtles look like?

The sloth replied, "I don't know, it all happened so fast!"

WHAT DO SLOTHS THROW IN THE WINTER?
Slowballs.

Ever hear the joke about the sloth crossing the road?

Never mind, it'd take too long.

WHAT DO YOU GET WHEN YOU CROSS A SLOTH WITH A PORCUPINE?
You get a slowpoke.

Sheep

What is a lamb's favorite karate move?
A lamb chop.

WHAT DO YOU CALL A SHEEP COVERED IN CHOCOLATE?
A Candy Baaaa.

What do you call a hundred sheep rolling down a hill?
A lamb-slide.

Pig

FUN FACT

Pigs are intelligent animals and are considered even smarter than dogs! Research scientists have even taught some pigs to play video games!

Knock, knock.
Who's there?
Pig
Pig who?
Pig on someone your own size!

What kind of work do piglets do after school?
Ham-work.

Why are pigs awful basketball players?
Because they aways **hog** the ball!

Alpaca

What do you call an alpaca with a carrot in each ear?

Anything you want. He can't hear you!

When does an alpaca go "moo?"

When it's learning a new language.

What did the alpaca say when she was invited on vacation?

Alpaca my bags!

Duck

What do ducks like with their soup? **Quackers!**

What time do ducks like to wake up?
The *quack* of dawn!

What did the duck use to fix things around his house?
Duck tape!

45

Hippopotamus

FUN FACT
Even though hippos spend up to 16 hours a day in the water, they can neither swim or float!

What kind of music makes hippos dance?
Hip-Hop

What did the little hippo call his father?
Hippo-*papa*-mus!

How can you tell if a hippopotamus is in the refrigerator?
The door won't close!

Tiger

FUN FACT
Tigers can imitate the calls of other animals!
Some tigers will mimic sounds made by their
prey to attract them and lure them into a trap!

Why do tigers have stripes?
So they don't get spotted!

How does the tiger greet the other
animals in the jungle?
"Nice to eat you!"

How do you catch a unique tiger?
Unique up on it.

How do you catch a tame tiger?
Tame way.

Sea Otter

What is the name of the famous book about a wizard otter?

Harry Otter!

Why did the otter want to be an astronaut?

She wanted to get to otter space.

What did the otter pup's mom say when he had been naughty?

You otter be ashamed of yourself!

Arctic Fox

FUN FACT
The arctic fox's fur changes colors with the seasons! They can be white, brown, or even blueish gray, depending on the time of year!

Why do foxes have winter coats?
Because they look silly in sweaters!

Where did the arctic fox keep her wallet and hairbrush?

In her designer *furse*.

What did the arctic fox say after hearing wonderful news?

ARE YOU FUR REAL?

Tree Frog

FUN FACT
Tree frogs use their bright colors to confuse predators and help them make a fast escape!

How does a tree frog feel when he has a broken leg?
Unhoppy!

Why are tree frogs never angry?
Because they eat whatever bugs them!

What do you get when you cross a tree frog and a rabbit?

A bunny *ribbit!*

Orangutan

WHY DO ORANGUTANS HAVE BIG NOSTRILS?
They have big fingers!

What do you feed a 200-pound orangutan for dinner?

Anything he wants!

Why did the orangutan go to the doctor?

 Her banana wasn't peeling well.

Beluga Whale

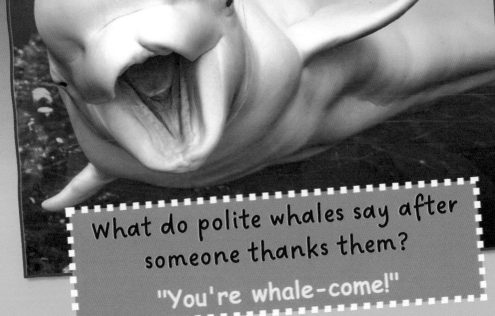

What do polite whales say after someone thanks them?

"You're whale-come!"

What did the whale yell to scare everyone?

"OOGA BELUGA!"

What did the whale say to his friend when he asked him to hang out?

"Might as whale."

FUN FACT
Goslings (baby geese) will bond with the first thing they see after hatching, other animals, humans, or even objects!

What do you get if you cross a cow and a goose?
A *mooooose!*

How can you tell if geese are scared?
They'll have goosebumps.

Why was the goose such a bad driver?
Because she honked at everything!

53

Jaguar

Why do jaguars eat their meat raw?
Because they don't know how to cook.

Why did the jaguar lose at poker?
Because he was playing with a *cheetah!*

Why are jaguars bad at
playing hide-and-seek?
Because they're always spotted!

Iguana

FUN FACT
Iguanas like to climb and spend time in the trees. They occasionally fall but usually land with no injuries even from great heights of 40-50 feet!

What did the vampire lizard say to his next victim?

I-guana suck your blood!

What do you call 100 iguanas falling out of a tree at the same time?

A lizard blizzard.

Seal

Why are seals so funny? Because they're the seal-iest animals!

What did the seal study in school? ART ART ART!!!

WHERE DO SEALS GO TO SEE MOVIES? At the dive-in theater.

Ostrich

Why are ostriches so strong?
They eggs-ercise!

What do you get if you try and kiss an ostrich?

A peck on the cheek!

Did you hear about the race between the giraffe and the ostrich?

It was neck and neck the whole way.

Panda

What's black and white and black and white and black and white?

A panda rolling down a hill.

What does a panda use to cook?
A pan. Duh!

What do pandas eat on Halloween?
BamBOO!

What is black and white
and red in places?
A sunburned panda!

Why do pandas like old movies?
Because they're in black and white.

Goldfish

DID YOU HEAR ABOUT THE GOLDFISH THAT WON SECOND PLACE?

He became a silverfish!

A man walks into a bakery with a goldfish in a bowl under his arm and says, "Do you have fish cakes?"

The lady behind the counter replies, "No".

"That's a shame," he says. "Today is his birthday."

Kookaburra

HOW DO YOU GET A KOOKABURRA TO STOP ITS CALLING?
Take away its cell phone.

WHAT DID THE KOOKABURRA SAY WHEN SHE WAS COLD?
Birrrrrrd!

WHY DID THE KOOKABURRA CROSS THE ROAD?
Because it was the chicken's day off!

Moray Eel

Why did the moray have to go to the doctor?
Because he was feeling pretty eel!

What kind of eels can travel on land?
Wheels!

What did the eel say to his friends when he was leaving their house?
Eel see ya later!

Camel

FUN FACT
Camels can go for weeks without a drink, but when they do, they can slurp up to 40 gallons of water in one go!

Why do camels blend in so well with their surroundings?

THEY USE CAMEL-FLAGE.

What did the camel directing a movie yell?

LIGHTS, CAMEL-RA, ACTION!

How did the camel cross the desert without going hungry?

Because of all the *sand*wiches he ate.

INDEX

Enjoy these other great books by JACK LEWIS:

Never Bring a Zebracorn to School

Joy to the World: The Best Christmas Gift Ever

Wonderful World of Animals Series
Take a trip around the world to find the wildest, weirdest, and most adorable animals on the planet!

The Cutest Animals of the World Book for Kids

The Weirdest Animals of the World Book for Kids

Dangerous Animals of the World Book for Kids

Funny Animals of the World Joke Book for Kids

Color and Learn Animals of the World Series
Entertaining, educational, and awesome coloring books about the most fascinating animals in the world!

The Cutest Animals of the World Coloring Book for Kids

The Weirdest Animals of the World Coloring Book for Kids

Dangerous Animals of the World Coloring Book for Kids

Today I Found... Series
Magical children's stories of friendship and the power of imagination!

Today I Found a Unicorn

Today I Found a Mermaid

Today I Found an Elf

Fun with Family Series
A wonderful way to celebrate each special person in our families!

I Love My Mommy

Printed in Great Britain
by Amazon

19409226R00038